D0419311

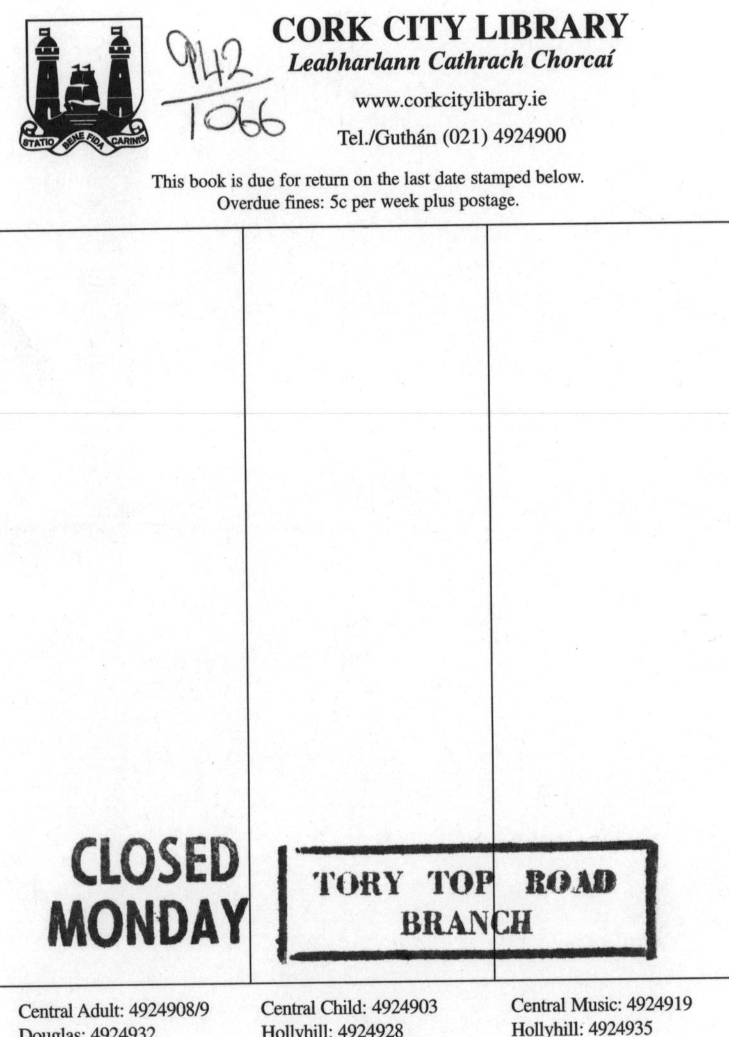
STATIO BENE FIDA CARINIS

Great Plague & Fire

London in Crisis

RICHARD TAMES

First published in Great Britain by Heinemann Library
Halley Court, Jordan Hill, Oxford OX2 8EJ
a division of Reed Educational & Professional Publishing Ltd.
Heinemann is a registered trademark of Reed Educational & Professional Publishing Ltd.

OXFORD FLORENCE PRAGUE MADRID ATHENS MELBOURNE AUCKLAND
KUALA LUMPUR SINGAPORE TOKYO IBADAN NAIROBI KAMPALA JOHANNESBURG
GABORONE PORTSMOUTH NH (USA) CHICAGO MEXICO CITY SAO PAOLO

Designed by Jim Evoy
Illustrations by Jeff Edwards
Printed in Hong Kong

04 03
10 9 8 7 6 5

ISBN 0 431 06878 X

British Library Cataloguing in Publication Data
Tames, Richard, 1946–
Great plague and fire: London in crisis. - (Turning points in history)
1. Plague - England - London - History - 17th century - Juvenile literature
2. Fires - England - London - History - 17th century - Juvenile literature
3. Great Britain - History - Charles II, 1660–1685 - Juvenile literature
I. Title
942.1'066

Acknowledgements
The Publishers would like to thank the following for permission to reproduce photographs:
Fotomas Index, pp. 9,14, 22, 27; Grace Collection at The British Library, p. 25;
Guildhall Library, pp. 7, 8, 21, 28; Magdalen College, pp.11, 15, 16; Mansell Collection, p. 17;
Museum of London, p. 19; National Portrait Gallery, p. 13;
Tames, Richard, pp. 4, 5, 6, 12, 20, 23, 24, 26, 29.

Cover photograph: Museum of London

Our thanks to Jane Shuter for her help in the preparation of this book.

Every effort has been made to contact copyright holders of any material reproduced in this book. Any omissions will be rectified in subsequent printings if notice is given to the Publisher.

Some words are shown in bold, **like this**. You can find out what they mean by looking in the glossary.

Contents

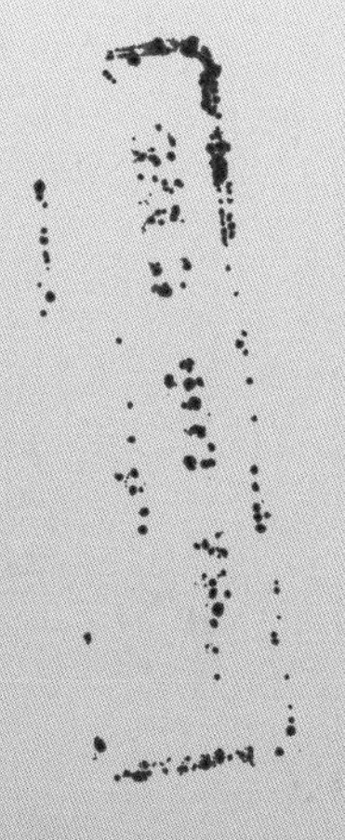

The unexpected and the accidental

Death of a city?

Great cities can overcome terrible disasters. London probably lost between a third and half its population when the plague known as the Black Death swept through Europe in 1348–9. But the city recovered and continued to grow despite repeated outbreaks of plague. Chicago was devastated by fire in 1871 but was quickly rebuilt. But suppose a city suffered both these catastrophes – one after the other? That was just what happened to London in 1665 and 1666.

The Great Plague

The Great Plague of 1665 was an unexpected turning point, not because plague was new, but because it was so much worse than ever before. Outbreaks of the disease happened every summer. Rich Londoners often fled to the country for safety. But, in 1665, so many people left, that London became a city of empty streets and a few frightened people.

Memento mori is Latin for 'reminder of death'. These spiked skulls are on the gate to St Olave's church, Hart Street, built in 1651.

FATAL FACTS

- In 1603, Edmund, younger brother of playwright William Shakespeare, came to join him in London. Within months Edmund died of plague.
- Poet John Milton's wife died after having their third child. A baby son also died. Milton's second wife also died after childbirth.
- In 1669, Samuel Pepys, a successful government official, treated his wife to a holiday abroad. She caught a fever and died, aged 29.

The Great Fire

Fires were common in cities with many wooden buildings. The Great Fire of 1666 became a major disaster because when it started it seemed no more than a nuisance – until it was too late. Afterwards, people asked what had caused these awful events. Were they punishments from God? Were they the work of an enemy? Or were they just accidents?

The Monument to the Great Fire of 1666. It is 60.6 metres high and 60.6 metres from where the fire started. It is a symbol of the re-birth of the City of London and was completed in 1677.

London

Britain's biggest

In 1660, London had a population of about 450,000, making it a hundred times larger than the average British market town. London's population was over five times as big as Britain's next five biggest cities – Norwich, Bristol, Newcastle, York and Exeter – combined. In all Europe only Paris was greater.

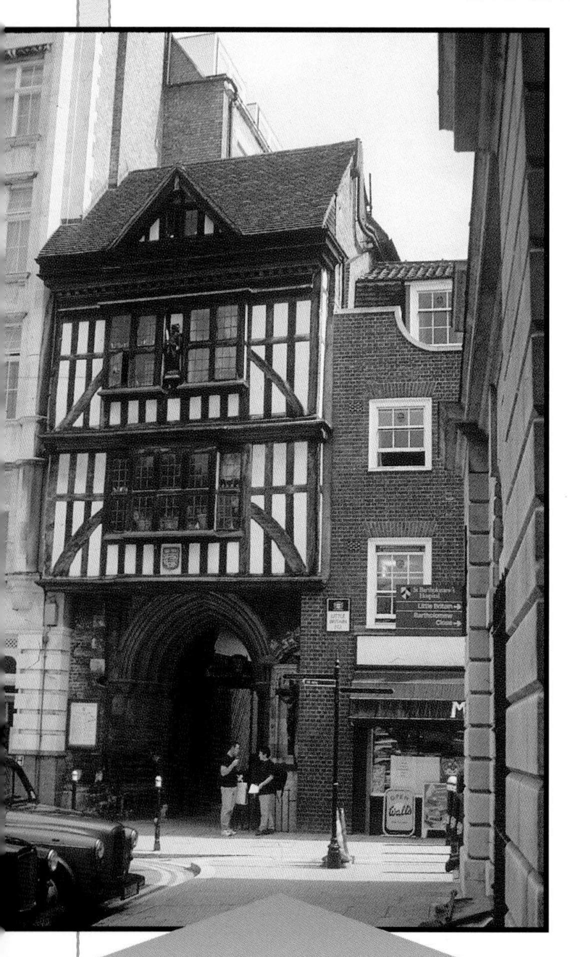

A rare survival from London before the Great Fire. This half-timbered gatehouse at the church of St Bartholomew the Great, Smithfield, dates from around 1550. The fire died out about a hundred metres away.

But, although London's churches and other public buildings were made of stone or brick, most ordinary homes, as well as shops and **warehouses** along the riverside, were still made of wood and thatch.

The City

London in 1665 had been growing rapidly, both in population and area, for over a century. The core area was the City of London proper, founded by the Romans around AD 50 and still surrounded by the walls and gates they first built. The Tower of London marked its eastern **boundary**. Outside the northern wall was marshy Moorfields, where young people skated in winter, and an open area, Smithfield, where a weekly horse-fair was held. To the west the city spilled over towards Holborn and Temple.

The suburbs

Around the City was an arc of **slums**, stretching from St Giles in the west, through Islington and Shoreditch to the north, and to Spitalfields and Whitechapel in the east.

A panoramic view of the western half of the City of London around 1610. Notice how the buildings were closely packed together, making it easy for the fire to spread.

The only bridge across the Thames was ancient London Bridge, dating from 1209. Lined with houses and shops, it was one of the wonders of the world. At its southern end was Southwark, the only built-up area on the south side of the river. A couple of miles upstream, around the bend of the Thames, stood Westminster and Whitehall, where King Charles II held his court. Beyond that lay quite separate villages, like Kensington and Chelsea.

Law and order

The City was governed by a Corporation, headed by the Lord Mayor, and **Aldermen** representing each of the 25 wards into which the city was divided. Many everyday matters were controlled by **parishes**, centred on local churches.

Considering its size London was a fairly law-abiding place. But not even Parliament could control its growth. Laws were passed repeatedly to ban the building or subdividing of houses but they were more often ignored than obeyed.

Sickness in the city

The Great Plague was the last in a series of plagues stretching back to the Black Death of 1348–9.

What was the Black Death?

The Black Death got its name from the soft, dark swellings in the armpits and groin which were the main signs of **infection**. The swellings, known as buboes, give it the modern name of bubonic plague.

How was it spread?

It was spread by fleas which had fed on the blood of a rodent – usually a rat – which had the disease. Plague **bacteria** breed inside the flea, building up a blockage in its digestive system. When the flea fed again, on another rat or a human, the blockage forced blood back into the bite, along with plague bacteria.
The first signs of illness – very high temperature, vomiting, pains in the muscles and **delirium** – appeared about a week after being bitten. Then came the buboes, which filled up with pus and became extremely painful. In 60 to 90 percent of cases where no modern medicines were available death followed within days.

Panic in the City. Londoners flee the plague in 1625 but are challenged by armed guards protecting surrounding areas.

Another form of plague

Pneumonic plague is caused by breathing in droplets of the infection from the lungs of someone who already has the bubonic form in an advanced stage. Pneumonic plague is even more deadly, spreads much more rapidly and almost always causes death in less than three days.

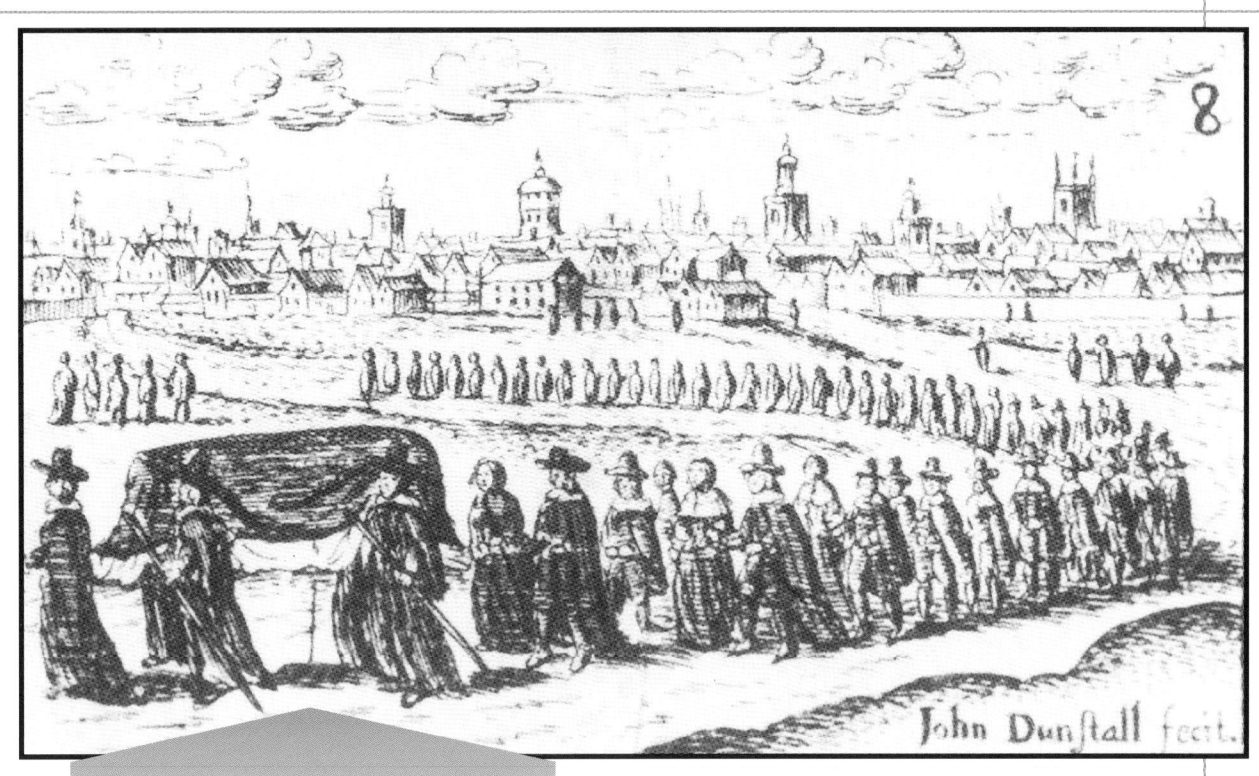

This picture shows an orderly funeral procession with many mourners. In reality regular burial arrangements often broke down during epidemics.

Where did it come from?

The Black Death of 1348–9 began in China, spread across Central Asia to the Black Sea and entered Europe by way of flea-bearing rats on Italian merchant ships coming back to the great ports of Venice and Genoa. It probably killed about one-third of the population of Europe.

Another major **epidemic** broke out in 1361. Why plague suddenly flared up and then died down for long periods after that depended on changes in climate and environment which favoured or limited its strength and that of the rat population.

LONDON - PLAGUE CITY

Ports, with many rat-infested ships constantly coming in from foreign countries, were especially likely to suffer repeated outbreaks of disease. In the century before the Great Plague of 1665 England's biggest port, London, suffered plague every ten to twenty years:-

Year	Deaths
1563	17,500
1578	6,000
1582	7,000
1593	18,000
1603	29,000
1609	4,200
1625	41,300
1636	10,000
1647	3,500

The stricken city

At Christmas 1664 Dr Nathaniel Hodges of Watling Street was 'called to a young man in a Fever, who after two days ... had two Risings about the bigness of a Nutmeg broke out, one on each thigh.' The patient recovered and, until spring, that was that. All London lay in the grip of a frost so hard the Thames itself froze solid.

The beginning

As the weather became warmer plague spread slowly in the western **suburbs**, especially St Giles and Covent Garden. Older men, remembering the 1647 outbreak, began sending their families to the country. But in May only a single death was recorded inside the city itself.

By early June, the **infection** was spreading south and west to Westminster, east through Holborn to the City proper and, round its northern edge, through Islington to Whitechapel. During the last week of June 725 people died, but still only 4 people died within the city walls.

This map shows where the plague was at its worst.

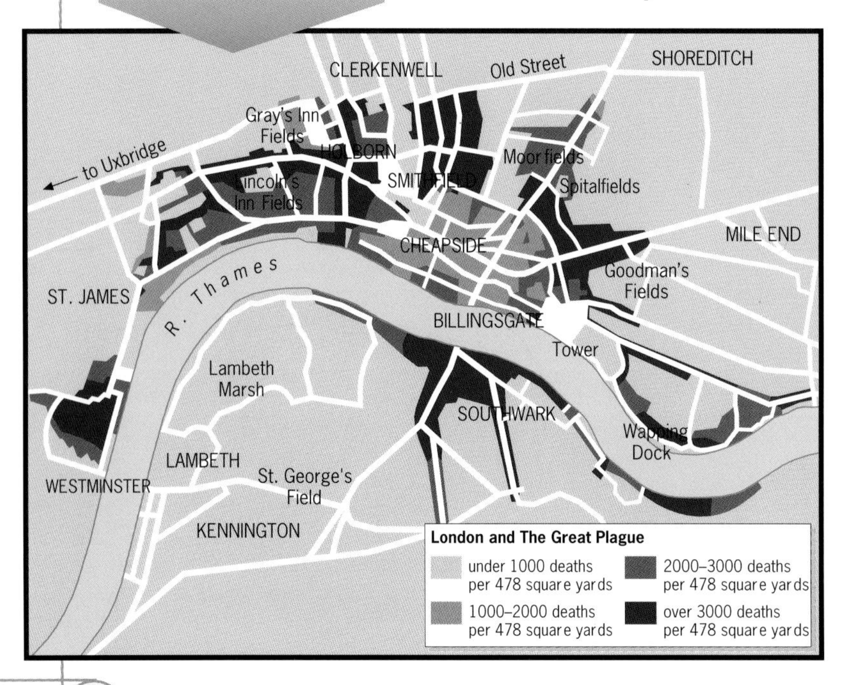

The peak

By mid-July, over 1000 people were dying every week. Panic seized the population.

- Parliament and the law courts closed.
- When people paid for goods, shopkeepers dipped the coins in vinegar because they thought they might carry infection.

- The royal family fled to Oxford, where less powerful **refugees** were turned away in case they were infected.
- At Guildford, Surrey, wells were padlocked to stop strangers using them.
- People in Dorchester were so terrified at finding a plague victim, they dug a huge pit and tipped into it the entire building he had died in, rather than touch the body.

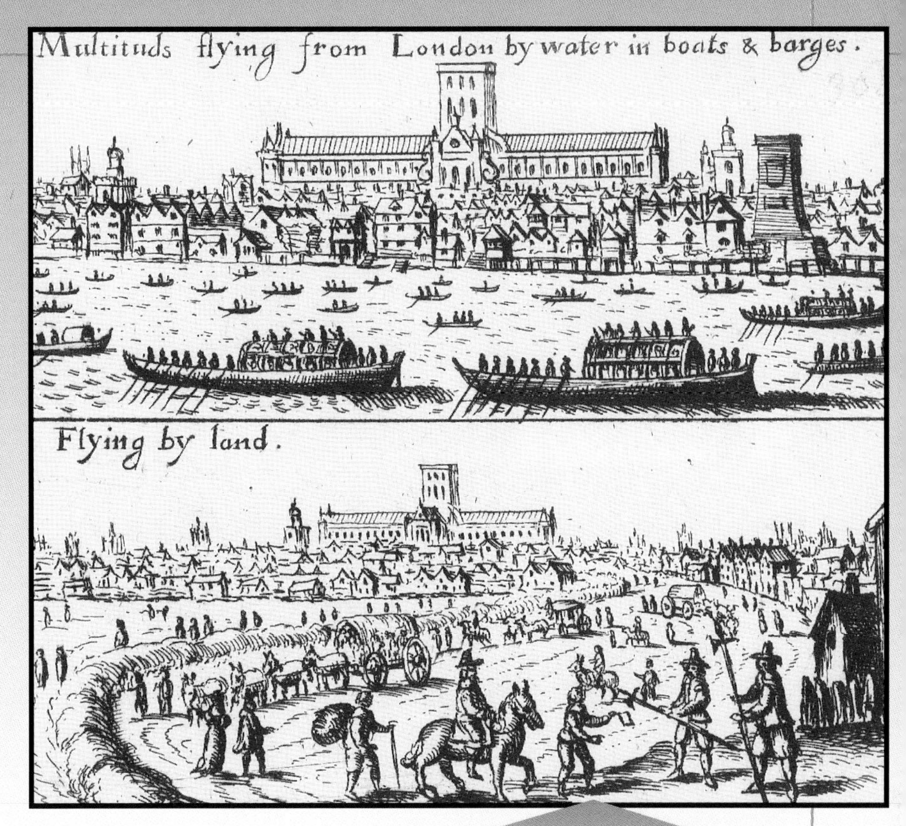

Londoners fleeing the City. In the bottom picture a man shows guards a certificate declaring him free of plague.

Early August

By early August, London's recorded weekly death-toll was over 2000. The **epidemic** peaked in the third week of September with 8297 deaths recorded.

DEATH'S DIARY

1665

March – winter frost ends
April – first cases of plague
May – June – suburbs infected
July – many rich desert London
September – plague deaths peak

1666

February – King returns

Autumn

As the weather turned colder the death-rate fell. By the end of November, it was down to 900. Refugees began to trickle back. But most businesses remained at a standstill and grass grew in the streets. Not until February 1666 did King Charles think it safe enough to return.

Eyewitness survivors: plague

Pepys the diarist

Samuel Pepys (1633–1703) was an important official who bought supplies for the Royal Navy. Here are some passages from his detailed diary of events in 1665:

7 June *the hottest day ever I felt in my life. Red crosses and 'Lord have mercy on us' being painted on houses.*

17 June *Coachman driving me suddenly passed out with fever.*

29 June *Visited Whitehall and saw the Court full of waggons and people ready to go out of town.*

29 July *The bell of St Olave's church, opposite my house, rings five or six times a day for funerals.*

10 August *Drew up a* ***will****, the town growing so unhealthy that a man cannot depend upon living two days to an end.*

12 August *The Lord Mayor has ordered every healthy person still in the city to be indoors by 9 pm so that the sick could take the cool evening air.*

31 August *Fled downriver to Woolwich, where I had already sent my wife for safety.*

Sunday *Went to church wearing my new wig. Wonder if plague affecting sales of wigs – many people believe they are now being made with hair from plague victims.*

This bust of Samuel Pepys stands near where his office was.

John Evelyn

Diarist John Evelyn was an eyewitness to both the plague and the fire. The skull in this picture is another *memento mori* (reminder of death).

John Evelyn (1620-1706) was a lifelong friend of Pepys, and also kept a diary, with even more detailed descriptions of what he saw.

He lived out at Deptford, not far from Woolwich where Pepys and his wife fled. Evelyn sent his family even further away, to Surrey. He stayed where he was because the king had put him in charge of looking after sailors taken prisoner in the war then being fought against the Dutch.

A month later Evelyn ventured into London:
..a dismal passage and dangerous. So many coffins exposed in the streets now thin of people and all in mournful silence, not knowing whose turn might be next.

Whenever his coach stopped he found himself surrounded by multitudes of poor begging **alms**.

In December he wrote:
Now blessed be God for his extraordinary mercies and preservation of me this year, when thousands and ten thousands perished, there dying in our ***parish*** *this year 406 of the pestilence!*

Fighting the plague

Plague and poverty

Seventeenth-century doctors did not understand what caused plague and had no effective way of treating it. Some blamed eating unripe fruit or food that had gone rotten. As plague usually occurred first among the poor, who had to eat whatever they could get, this probably seemed a reasonable theory. Even more doctors believed plague was caused by foul air arising from stinking piles of garbage, another regular feature of **slum** life.

In fact the link between plague and poverty was more to do with living in filthy huts and hovels, surrounded by donkeys, pigs and chickens. This created an ideal breeding-ground for rats carrying plague-bearing fleas.

Quarantine, fire and massacre

The governments of Italian ports learned that sometimes plague could be kept at bay by forcing suspected ships to wait offshore for 40 days until they were clearly not **infected** or the outbreak was over. The Italian word for forty, *quaranta*, gave a name for this procedure – quarantine.

A family locked up in their house under quarantine.

During the Great Plague the first steps taken by the Lord Mayor of London were to order all visitors to leave the City and all sufferers to be locked in their houses, under armed guard, with all their family and servants, until they had either recovered or died.

Carrying a coffin through Covent Garden. The normally busy market is completely deserted. Notice that all the officials carry staves for handling corpses, as a sign of their office, and to warn off other people.

A red cross was painted on the door to warn off others. Pepys's own doctor died after being shut up for a month.

A harmless remedy

As things got worse orders were given to burn massive bonfires in the streets to make the air 'pure'. This was useless. But burning a mixture of sulphur, saltpetre and amber inside individual houses did work. It did not kill the infection, as people thought, but it did keep the rats away.

Finally it was decided that the sickness was being spread by household pets. Pepys estimated that 40,000 dogs and 200,000 cats were clubbed or poisoned to death. In fact this was the worst thing to do because dogs and cats killed the rats which were the creatures really responsible for spreading the disease.

Safety in flight

The best hope of survival lay in leaving London and getting as far away as possible. About 10,000 people also took to boats anchored in the middle of the river. Most of them survived.

Bring out your dead!

Pest houses and plague pits

Many doctors and priests fled. Those staying to treat or comfort the dying often paid with their lives. Pest houses for plague victims were built on the outskirts of London, in Marylebone, Soho and Stepney. The people in charge were paid £2 per patient whether they lived or died, so it suited them to have as many die as quickly as possible.

Churchyards used for burials were soon overflowing, so mass graves were dug. As the supply of coffins ran out, corpses were just flung into pits. Collecting bodies was highly dangerous but there were plenty of **volunteers**. Some believed they were immune to plague. Some wanted to steal from the dead. Others were starving for lack of other work.

City at a standstill

The ships which normally brought coal from Newcastle refused to land. Businesses closed down for lack of fuel. Rich people fleeing London often left servants behind to fend for themselves. Gangs of **unemployed** roamed the streets, robbing, or breaking into abandoned houses to loot them.

Burying the dead in pits. As the plague reached its peak it was no longer possible to arrange individual burials in coffins.

How many died?

The **parish** clerk at St Olave's, where Pepys worshipped, told him that *'There died nine this week, though I have returned only six.'* Parish clerks compiled the weekly Bills of Mortality recording causes of death. They listed many plague deaths as being caused by *'wind'*, *'convulsion'*, *'worms'* or *'griping in the guts'*. Partly this was to calm public fears, partly so that the relatives of the dead would not be locked up as **infected** persons.

In any case causes of death were reported, not by doctors, but by uneducated old women 'searchers' who could easily be **bribed**. In all, the Bills listed 68,576 plague victims. Nearly another 7000 deaths from 'Spotted Fever' should almost certainly be added to this figure. The true total is probably over 80,000 and perhaps as many as 100,000 people died from the plague.

During the plague of 1625 the poet John Taylor wrote:
*'All trades are dead, or almost out of breath
But such as live by sickness and by death.'*
Pepys described how he *'could find neither meat nor drink. My brewer's house is shut up, and my baker, with his whole family, dead of the Plague.'*
The Rev. Thomas Vincent noted the silence of the streets. *'No prancing horses, no rattling coaches, no calling on customers nor offering wares. If any voice be heard it is the groans of dying persons.'*

MEMENTO MORI

LONDON'S Dreadful Visitation:
Or, A COLLECTION of All the
Bills of Mortality
For this Present Year:
Beginning the 27th of December 1664. and
ending the 19th. of December following:
As also, The GENERAL or whole years BILL:
According to the Report made to the
KING's Most Excellent Majesty,
By the Company of Parish-Clerks of London. &c.

LONDON:
Printed and are to be sold by E. Cotes living in Aldersgate-street.
Printer to the said Company 1665.

The London Bills of Mortality for the plague year – a special report prepared for King Charles II. Notice the hour-glasses and grave diggers' tools – symbols of passing time and death.

London ablaze

Sunday, 2 September

Just before 2 am, a workman in Thomas Farynor's bakery in Pudding Lane was woken by smoke and heat from its oven. Farynor and his family escaped over the roof-tops. Soon afterwards the **parish** constable and nightwatchmen reported the fire to the Lord Mayor, Sir Thomas Bludworth. He looked out of his bedroom window but thought it was just a small fire and went back to bed.

By seven in the morning, 300 houses had burned down. Fanned by a fierce east wind, the fire was spreading onto London Bridge itself. By that night, the blaze was over a mile long.

Monday, 3 September

The river front west of London Bridge was now burning furiously. The Royal Exchange, the centre of the City's business life, burned down. St Paul's Cathedral, encased in wooden scaffolding for repairs, began to blaze.

How the fire spread

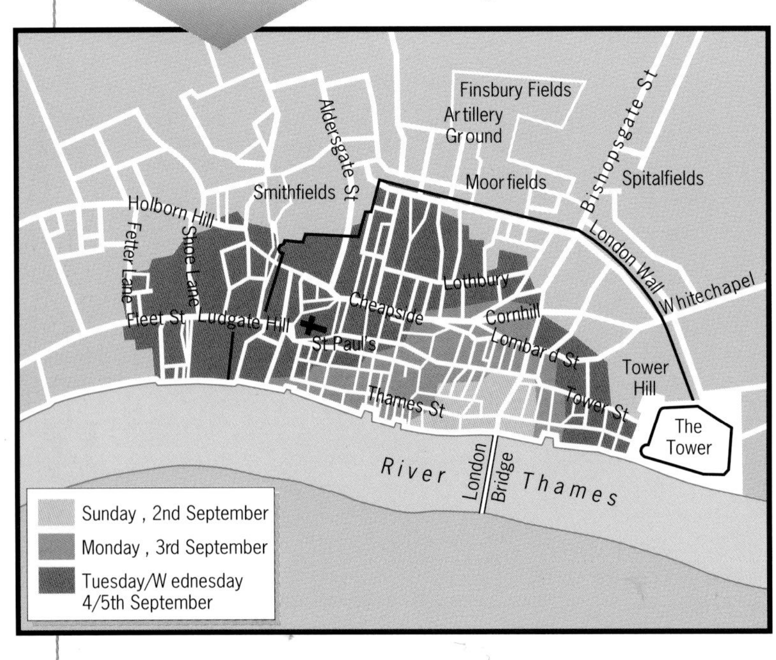

Tuesday, 4 September

Half the entire City was now in flames. Cheapside, the City's main shopping street, was wiped out. Guildhall, seat of the city's government, went next. Still the fire drove westwards, leaping the Fleet River to burn half way up Fleet Street itself.

This picture of the fire was painted by a Dutch artist soon after the event. He was probably not an eyewitness but relied on engravings of London as it was before the event.

Wednesday, 5 September

The fire reached Temple and Cripplegate, but then the wind dropped and it stopped just short of Smithfield and Holborn.

THE DAMAGE

- 1666 – more of City of London destroyed by fire than by German bombers in the 1940–1 Blitz
- 151 hectares (over half total area) burned out within city walls
- 25 hectares burned out outside city walls
- 13,200 houses on 400 streets up in flames
- 87 churches and most major public buildings gone
- 100,000 people to spend winter in tents and makeshift shelters
- £10,000,000 – estimated value of goods and property destroyed
- Height of flames – up to 100 metres (ten times height of a three-storey house)
- Death toll – only eight people (most fled rather than fight such a fire)

Eyewitness survivors: fire

Pepys again

Sunday, 2 September *brought news of fire to King Charles II at Westminster (round bend in river, out of sight of the disaster)*

Monday, 3 September *At 4 am I packed my money and silverware onto a cart and rode 2 miles east of London, to Bethnal Green to leave my things at a friend's house.*

Tuesday, 4 September *Dug a pit in the garden of my house and buried my store of wine and Parmesan cheese for safekeeping.*

From tower of All Hallows Church saw everywhere great fires. The wind had dropped but there was still a blaze at the Temple, Holborn and Cripplegate, where the King himself was seen helping the soldiers.

Cruel fate

As it happened, Pepys' own house was spared – but burned down in another fire seven years later.

Pepys brings news of the fire to King Charles II – a mural painted in the 1990s

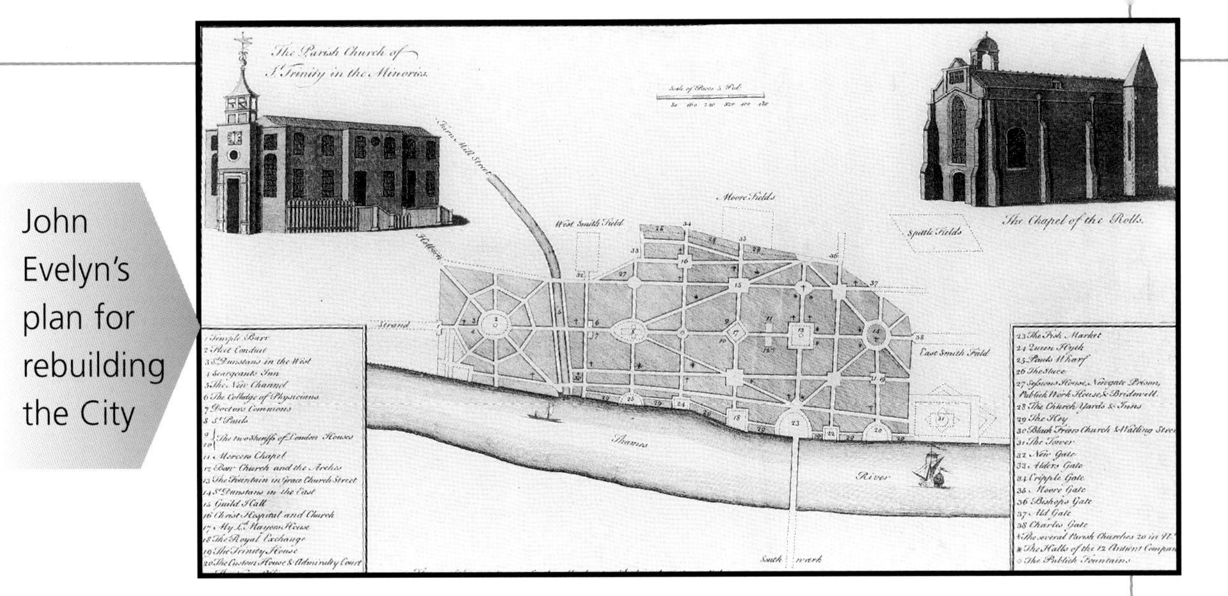

John Evelyn's plan for rebuilding the City

John Evelyn too

King Charles II put Evelyn in charge of a firefighting team at Fetter Lane, Holborn. Here are some extracts from his diary:

Sunday, 2 September *It was light as day for ten miles round about.*

Tuesday, 4 September *Worst day of fire. The stones of St Paul's flew like grenades, the lead (from its roof) melting down the streets in a stream and the very pavements glowing with fiery redness so as no horse, nor man was able to tread on them.*

He explained why the fire got out of control:

The conflagration was so universal and the people so astonished that from the beginning they hardly stirred to quench it, so as there was nothing heard or seen but crying out and running about like distracted creatures. God grant mine eyes may never behold the like, who now saw above 10,000 houses all in one flame. The shrieking of women and children, the hurry of people, the fall of towers, houses and churches, was like a hideous storm.

When he returned a week later to Holborn he wrote:

I went again to the ruins, for it was now no longer a city. London was, but is no more. The poor inhabitants were dispersed, some under tents, some under miserable huts and hovels, many without a rag or any utensils. From riches and well-furnished houses people were now reduced to extremist misery.

Fighting the fire

Equipment and methods

Because fires were frequent in a London of wooden buildings, each city ward had a store of hooked poles, axes and chains for pulling down burning thatch, or demolishing a whole house if necessary. There were also primitive pumps and squirts which could douse small flames. These were used during a big fire in 1633 but to little effect. The only ways to stop a major fire were to either blow up buildings with gunpowder to create gaps too big for the fire to cross, or to organize chains of firefighters passing buckets from a river or pond to the fire itself.

The Lord Mayor

Because the fire broke out in the night, few people were alert enough to tackle it quickly. By the time Lord Mayor Bludworth ordered **parish** constables and watchmen into action on Sunday, 2 September it was already too late. Pepys, returning from Westminster, gave him the king's orders to pull down houses. Bludworth cried despairingly *'Lord what can I do? I am spent, people will not obey me. I have been pulling down houses but the fire overtakes us faster than we can do it.'*

This engraving of the Great Fire was probably done about a century later. It is correct in showing how only a few stone and brick buildings resisted the flames.

The blazing Thames shoreline, stacked with timber, tar, rope and other combustibles, cut firefighters off from the city's main source of water. Fire on London Bridge cut off help from Southwark.

Londoners despair of fighting the fire – a mural of the 1990s

Dithering

Although it was clear by Monday that the City was facing a major catastrophe, neither the Lord Mayor nor the King himself was willing to take sole responsibility for destroying very large numbers of houses ahead of the fire's leading edge to make a fire-break. This delay ensured that the area west of Queenhithe, where they met to discuss this plan, burned down anyway.

Decisiveness

The King did, however, get his brother James, Duke of York to organize sailors, soldiers, constables and **volunteers** into teams of firefighters. By pulling down houses and organizing bucket-chains they were finally able to turn back the flames as the wind died away on Wednesday, 6 September. Sailors also saved the Tower of London by blowing up houses to make a fire-break. Through it all the King and Duke were bravely on the front line, encouraging volunteers to join in by handing out handfuls of cash, and fighting the flames shoulder to shoulder with them.

The aftermath

Arson or accident?

In April 1666, a number of Catholics had been hanged for allegedly plotting to burn London down on 3, September 1665. Even while the fire was raging Charles II had Frenchmen, Dutchmen and Catholics locked up for their own protection.

The statue of The Golden Boy at Pye Corner, Smithfield, marks where the fire ended at the north-east edge of the City. The inscription underneath said the disaster was God's punishment for the sin of gluttony – because it had started in Pudding Lane and ended at Pye Corner.

A MAD MAN CONFESSES

Immediately after the fire a Frenchman, Hubert, confessed to starting it. The courtier Lord Clarendon recorded that *'he was only accused on his own confession. Neither the judges nor any at the trial did believe him guilty, but that he was a distracted wretch, weary of his life.'* He was hanged anyway, but it was later proved that Hubert had not even arrived in London until two days after the fire began.

The reason why

Because the fire started in a baker's shop in Pudding Lane and ended near Smithfield at Pye Corner, an **inscription** was put up there saying that it had been God's punishment for the sin of gluttony. When Parliament set up a committee to report on the fire it concluded that the causes were *'the hand of God upon us, a great wind and the season so very dry.'*

A city purified?

Because London was never again visited by plague after 1666 many came to believe that the **infection** had somehow been burned out.

This ignores the fact that the **slum** areas where the plague had been worst, from St Giles in the west round to Whitechapel in the east, were untouched by the fire. Even more important is the fact that other British cities, which had no such fire, also became free of plague. Its decline was probably due to a change in climate or environment which affected its strength, or that of the rat population which carried it.

1669 engraving by John Leake shows the ruins of the City of London.

A safer city

It is probably still true that the rebuilding of the city in brick, stone and tile, rather than wood and thatch, with wider streets, proper pavements and better drains, did make it a healthier place. Even so, plenty of other diseases remained to threaten citizens and their families, most notably smallpox. The Foundling Hospital was established in 1742 as London's first orphanage. In its first year a third of the children admitted to it died. So children were sent out to the countryside to be fostered until they were five and likely to survive being brought back to London for their education and training.

The great rebuilding

The destruction of medieval London, with its narrow alleys and dank, dark courtyards, presented an historic opportunity to rebuild it on a grand scale.

A planned city?

King Charles II had seen the magnificent building of his cousin King Louis XIV of France in Paris and Versailles. Bold plans for reconstruction were drawn up within weeks by John Evelyn, mathematician Robert Hooke and astronomer Christopher Wren. But, unlike Louis XIV, Charles II had neither the power nor the money to order Londoners to give up their properties for the sake of some masterplan. Instead, the King and City Corporation appointed **commissioners**, including Wren and Hooke, to draw up building regulations and supervise the reconstruction of houses and business which Londoners would have to finance for themselves.

Over a hundred streets and lanes were widened and two new thoroughfares – King Street and Queen Street – built to link Guildhall with the Thames. Houses on main roads had to have four floors, on side roads three and in back streets two, plus **garrets** in the roof.

The Monument shows Charles II (right, with hand on hip and long wig) overseeing the rebuilding of London. Above hovers the spirit of prosperity pouring down the fruits of trade.

Rebuilding

A special Fire Court of 22 judges was set up to decide who owned what as the smoking wreckage was cleared away from the sites of former homes, shops and gardens. It sat until 1673.

In 1676, **surveyors,** Ogilby and Morgan completed the first, accurate modern map of London, on a scale of 100 feet to 1 inch (30m : 2.5cm). A tax on coal brought into London by sea raised £736,000 to fund improvements to the waterfront, the dredging and banking of the Fleet River and the rebuilding of Guildhall, St Paul's, the Royal Exchange and **parish** churches. Craftsmen flooded in from the countryside and abroad knowing they could find enough work for a lifetime. A year after the fire only 150 new buildings had been completed. But by 1671, 9000 houses were up, though more than a third remained empty. Work on St Paul's Cathedral did not even begin until 1675.

Soho Square – typical of the elegant West End squares built after the Great Fire.It is still there today.

West End, East End

By making 100,000 Londoners homeless, the Great Fire boosted the development of the West End for the rich and the East End for the poor. The wealthy moved to St James's, Soho and Bloomsbury, within walking distance of royal palaces and parks. The poor crowded into Spitalfields and Tower Hamlets, where rents were much lower than in rebuilt City houses.

Phoenix city

The master builder

Wren was an Oxford professor at 29. The only trip he ever made abroad, to Paris, saved him from the Great Plague and inspired him to become an architect. The Great Fire gave him a lifetime's work. He rebuilt St Paul's and 52 **parish** churches. Outside the City he designed three more churches, the Royal Observatory at Greenwich and the Royal Hospital, Chelsea and made major alterations to the royal palaces at Kensington and Hampton Court.

When it was completed in 1677, The Monument towered over its surroundings.

Newcomers

In 1685, Louis XIV drove 80,000 of his Protestant subjects out of France because of their religious beliefs. Most were highly skilled craftsmen, such as silversmiths and clockmakers. Half of them settled around London, in Soho, Spitalfields and Wandsworth, which quickly became industrial **suburbs** specializing in silk-weaving and making hats, paper, furniture and mirrors. These and other immigrants from Belgium and Italy added greatly to London's prosperity.

City institutions

The Great Fire boosted interest in the idea of insurance against disaster. Lloyd's of London, the world's most famous insurance company, grew out of the coffee house managed by Edward Lloyd. England's first regular newspapers were started to provide news of shipping and cargoes in this new market.

St Paul's - the second largest cathedral in Europe after St Peter's in Rome. Rebuilding St Paul's began in 1675 and was completed in 1710.

In 1694, the founding of the Bank of England marked an important new phase in the financing of government and business. By 1700, London, with a population of 575,000 was surpassing Paris as the first city of Europe. Neither plague nor fire could destroy London in the end – the city that refused to die.

'I WILL RISE AGAIN'

Christopher Wren's son recorded how his father began the rebuilding of St Paul's:
'When the SURVEYOR in Person had set out, upon the Place, the Dimensions of the great Dome, and fixed upon the Centre: a common Labourer was ordered to bring a flat stone from the Heaps of Rubbish to be laid for a Mark and Direction to the Masons; the Stone happened to be a Piece of Grave-Stone, with nothing remaining of the Inscription but this simple word in large capitals, 'RESURGAM.'
Resurgam is Latin for 'I will rise again'.
Wren, a deeply religious man, took this as a sign from God that he would live long enough to complete the huge task of rebuilding the Cathedral. He had '*Resurgam*' carved on the building above the figure of a phoenix, the legendary bird which, like London, was reborn from its own ashes.

Time-line

1348–49	The Black Death
1361	Second major outbreak of Black Death
1603, 1625, 1636, 1647	Major outbreaks of plague
1620	Birth of John Evelyn
1632	Birth of Sir Christopher Wren
1633	Birth of Samuel Pepys Major fire in London
1642	Outbreak of Civil War
1649	Execution of Charles I
1660	Charles II restored to throne
1665	March – winter frost ends May – first death from plague in City July – large-scale flight of population from London September – plague deaths reach their peak November – Londoners begin to return to the city
1666	February – Charles II and his court return to London from Oxford September 2–5 Great Fire of London
1673	The Fire Court finishes settling disputes about property rights and boundaries
1675	Reconstruction of St Paul's Cathedral begins
1676	Ogilby and Morgan's map of London published
1677	Completion of The Monument to the Great Fire
1685	Death of Charles II French Protestants flee to England
1694	Bank of England founded
1703	Death of Samuel Pepys
1706	Death of John Evelyn
1710	St Paul's Cathedral completed
1723	Death of Sir Christopher Wren

Glossary

Alderman	an official chosen to govern a part of the City of London and speak for it at meetings of the City Corporation
alms	money given to the poor
arson	starting a fire on purpose
bacteria	single-celled organism that may cause disease
boundary	line dividing one area from another
bribe	money given to a person to get them to do something they would not do otherwise
commissioner	an appointed official
delirium	a fevered state in which a person loses control of their normal senses
epidemic	many cases of the same disease happening at one time
garret	an attic
infection	catching a sickness
inscription	writing or carving to record an event
parish	area where people attending a particular church live
refugee	someone forced to leave their normal home or country
slum	area of bad housing
suburb	area on the edge of a city
surveyor	expert on measuring land and buildings
unemployed	not having work
volunteer	someone who does something willingly
warehouse	building where goods are stored, often by a river
will	legal document setting out who gets a person's property when they die

Index